STEP-BY-STEP

Hot and Cold Sandwiches

Hot and Cold Sandwiches

CAROL BOWEN

||| •PARRAGON• |||

First published in Great Britain in 1994 by
Parragon Book Service Ltd
4 Mulberry Close
Rosslyn Hill
Hampstead
London
NW3 5UP

ISBN 1 85813 926 0

Printed in Italy

Acknowledgements:

Design & DTP: Pedro & Frances Prá-Lopez / Kingfisher Design
Art Direction: Lisa Tai
Editor: Linda Doeser Publishing Services
Special Photography: Amanda Heywood
Home Economist: Nicola Fowler
Stylist: Marian Price

Gas Hob supplied by New World Domestic Appliances Ltd
Photographs on pages 6, 20, 34, 48, 62: Tony Stone Images

Note:
Cup measurements in this book are for American cups. Tablespoons are assumed to be 15ml.

Contents

CHAPTER ONE

Hot Sandwiches

Grilled, toasted, baked or fried, hot sandwiches are equally ideal for the solitary diner or football club. However, to be enjoyed at their best they should be eaten the moment they emerge from the pan, toaster or oven.

This may be a problem when catering for large numbers. Have your grilled, toasted and 'filled for the oven' sandwich combinations prepared well ahead, perhaps in the freezer or the refrigerator ready for cooking. There is no need to thaw frozen sandwiches for toasting or grilling – they become particularly light and crispy when toasted straight from the freezer. Enlist the aid of a helper – this is definitely a two-person operation!

Fried sandwiches, such as the classic Croque Monsieur, are lusciously rich and make a warming snack or appetizing lunch or supper dish. They need to be cooked quickly so timing is crucial. This ensures that the filling will melt, as the bread becomes crisp and golden brown. For best results, fry in a mixture of butter and oil; the butter adds flavour while the oil enables a high enough temperature to be reached for crisp results. Drain on absorbent kitchen paper and serve while still piping hot!

Opposite: *There are numerous varieties of hot sandwich fillings that one can prepare indoors or out!*

STEP 2

STEP 3

STEP 5

STEP 6

ITALIAN HEROES

These are long, crusty rolls that are split in half lengthwise, topped with an onion and green pepper mixture, then covered with hot Italian sausages.

SERVES 4

12 Italian sausages
4 tbsp water
2 tbsp olive or vegetable oil
2 onions, sliced
4 or 5 red or green peppers, or a mixture of
*   both, cored and cut into strips*
4 long, crusty hero-type rolls

1 Put the sausages in a pan with the water. Cover and simmer gently for about 5 minutes. Remove the lid and continue to cook for about 15 minutes or until the sausages are browned, turning them occasionally.

2 Meanwhile, heat the oil in another pan and sauté the sliced onions for about 5–8 minutes until they are soft but not coloured.

3 Add the pepper strips and continue cooking, stirring occasionally, for about 10 minutes or until the peppers are tender.

4 Add the sausages and cook for a further 3 minutes.

5 Split the rolls in half lengthways. Spoon some of the cooked pepper and onion mixture onto the bottom half of each roll.

6 Top each roll base with three of the sausages, then replace the top half of each roll. Cut each roll in half crossways to serve.

ITALIAN SAUSAGES

Choose from meaty frying sausages such as *luganega*, spicy pork sausages from Romagna in the north (*salsiccia al metro*), which are sold in lengths; or *salamelle*, small, spicy sausages linked in a chain. Although the Italians would make these rolls spicy by using hot sausages, you may like to use plain sausages then spice up the onion mixture by adding 1-2 tbsp sun-dried or plain tomato purée mixed with a generous pinch of chilli powder or a dash of chilli sauce.

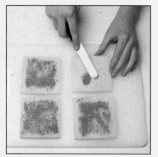

STEP 1

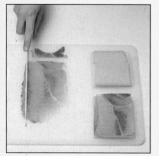

STEP 2

STEP 4

STEP 6

CROQUE MONSIEUR

This classic French sandwich is usually fried in butter and oil.
Here is a neater way to cook it – in the oven.

SERVES 4

8 thick slices white bread, crusts removed
prepared mustard, to taste
100 g/4 oz Gruyère cheese, sliced
100 g/4 oz cooked ham, thinly sliced
40 g/1½oz/3 tbsp butter, melted

1 Heat the oven to 230°C, 450°F, Gas Mark 8. Spread half of the slices of white bread with mustard to taste. (Dijon mustard is the traditional choice, but you may prefer to use a hotter mustard, or one of the many herbed mustard varieties that are now widely available.)

2 Trim the cheese slices to fit and put them on the bread. Trim the ham slices to fit and place them on top of the cheese.

3 Top with the remaining slices of bread to make sandwiches, and place them on a baking sheet.

4 Brush the sandwiches lightly with some of the melted butter, setting the remaining butter aside.

5 Cook in the top of the oven for about 5 minutes or until lightly browned. Turn the sandwiches over with a spatula, brush with the remaining butter and cook for a further 3–5 minutes.

6 Cut the sandwiches in half and serve them hot, wrapped in small paper napkins. Garnish with salad leaves if desired.

ADAPTING CROQUE MONSIEUR

Brown or wholegrain bread can be used instead of white bread to create Croque Monsieur, if you prefer. You may even like to add tomato slices.

If you prefer to cook these sandwiches on the hob, then fry in 50 g/ 2 oz/¼ cup butter with 2 tsp olive or corn oil until golden brown on both sides – about 1-2 minutes. Drain well on absorbent kitchen paper (paper towels) before halving to serve as above.

PO'-BOY SANDWICH

Generally battered and deep-fried, here the oysters are simply grilled (broiled) and served with a garlic and herb dressing.

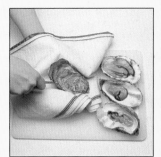

STEP 1

SERVES 4

16 fresh oysters
3 tbsp olive oil
25 g/1 oz/2 tbsp unsalted butter
1 clove garlic, crushed
1 tbsp chopped fresh parsley
freshly ground black pepper
1 tsp lemon juice
4 rashers streaky bacon, rinds removed
2 small (demi) baguettes, or French loaves
Tabasco sauce

1 Grill the oysters, flat shells uppermost, until the shells open slightly. The oyster liquid will start to bubble out of the shells after about 3–5 minutes. Hold the oysters in a cloth, insert a knife between the shells and twist off the top shell. Slip the knife under the oyster to release it from the bottom shell. Put the oysters in a bowl with their juices.

2 Stretch the bacon with the back of a knife, cut each rasher into 4 pieces and make 4 small bacon rolls from each.

3 Heat the oil and butter with the garlic in a small pan. Add the parsley, black pepper to taste and lemon juice, mixing well.

4 Thread the oysters and bacon rolls onto 4 lightly oiled skewers. Brush with the buttery sauce and grill (broil) for 2 minutes on each side, basting frquently until cooked.

5 Halve each baguette lengthways, and toast the cut sides until golden. Drizzle with the remaining garlic oil mixture.

6 Remove the oysters and bacon from the skewers and arrange on the bread. Sprinkle a little Tabasco sauce on top and serve at once.

STEP 2

STEP 3

A SOUTHERN CLASSIC

This is the famous Louisiana sandwich, packed with any number of fillings, from the more usual ham, cheese and turkey to soft-shelled crab and oysters. So experiment with your favourite fillings.

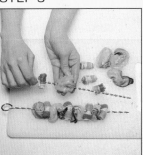

STEP 4

STEP 1

STEP 2

STEP 4

STEP 5

FRIED REUBEN SANDWICH

These sandwiches are made of rye bread, stuffed fit to burst with salt (corned) beef and sauerkraut, and fried until crisp and golden. They satisfy even man-sized appetites!

SERVES 4

6 tbsp mayonnaise
1 tbsp finely chopped green pepper
1 tbsp mild chilli sauce
8 slices rye bread
225 g/8 oz canned or bottled sauerkraut
75 g/3 oz Gruyère or Emmenthal (Swiss) cheese
225 g/8 oz salt (corned) beef, sliced
50 g/2 oz/¼ cup butter or margarine
1 tbsp oil

1 Mix the mayonnaise with the chopped green pepper and chilli sauce, blending well.

2 Spread about 1 tablespoon of the pepper mixture onto each slice of rye bread.

3 Drain the sauerkraut and slice the cheese into 8 pieces.

4 Place a piece of cheese (sliced quite thickly) on four slices of the bread. Top each slice with a quarter of the salt (corned) beef and a quarter of the sauerkraut. Cover each with another slice of cheese, then sandwich together with the remaining slices of bread, mayonnaise side down.

5 Melt the butter or margarine and oil in a large, heavy-based frying-pan. Add the sandwiches one by one and cook on one side for about 3–4 minutes until golden. Turn over and cook for a further 3–4 minutes until crisp and brown.

6 Drain on absorbent kitchen paper (paper towels). Cut in half and serve at once, garnished with sliced gherkins if desired.

A MILD CHANGE

Not surprisingly, these sandwiches originated in Germany, where chilli sauce was not part of the original recipe. If you have a sensitive palate, you may wish to leave out the chilli sauce for a milder flavour.

ITALIAN MOZZARELLA LOAF

This is a delicious pull-apart type of sandwich that makes a welcome appearance on the cold buffet table or at an outdoor barbecue when the weather turns a little chilly!

STEP 1

SERVES 4–6

1 tsp oil
1 x 450 g/1 lb rye and caraway seed loaf, not sliced
225 g/8 oz mozzarella cheese
50 g/2 oz/¼ cup butter, softened
10–12 anchovy fillets
12 black olives, halved and stoned
½ tsp dried marjoram
1 tsp fresh chopped basil or ½ tsp dried

1 Heat the oven to 220°C, 425°F, Gas Mark 7. Lightly grease a baking sheet with the oil. On a bread board, slice the loaf of bread at 2.5 cm/ 1 inch intervals almost through to the base, being careful not to cut it all the way through.

2 Cut the mozzarella into thin slices and insert each slice between the slices of bread.

3 Using a flat-bladed knife, spread the top of the loaf of bread with the softened butter.

4 Place the anchovies over the top of the bread in a criss-cross pattern. Scatter the olives on top and sprinkle with the herbs.

5 Place the loaf on the greased baking sheet and bake in the oven for 15 minutes until it is crisp and golden brown, and the cheese is bubbly.

6 Allow the loaf to stand for a few minutes before serving. Pull the slices of bread apart to eat.

STEP 2

STEP 3

MARINATED OLIVES

It is easy to marinate your own olives, for added flavour in this recipe. Drain a jar of black olives and place in a clean screwtop jar. Add peeled garlic cloves, orange rind and a sprig of fresh rosemary or thyme. Add olive oil to just cover the olives, cover the jar and leave the olives to marinate for at least a day.

STEP 4

STEP 1

STEP 2

STEP 3

STEP 4

CHEESE SHRIMPY

This is a Danish oven-baked open sandwich that is ideal to serve for a light supper or as a first course to a meal.

SERVES 2

75 g/ 3 oz semi-hard cheese, such as Samsoe
    or Edam
175 g/6 oz/1 cup peeled shrimps (small
    prawns)
2 tbsp mayonnaise
1 tbsp soured cream or natural yoghurt
juice of ¹/₂ lemon
salt and pepper
40 g/1¹/₂ oz/ 3 tbsp butter
4 slices close-textured white Danish bread
2 egg whites
parsley sprigs and 4 unpeeled shrimps
    (prawns), to garnish

1 Heat the oven to 200°C, 400°F, Gas Mark 6. Grate the cheese and set aside, together with a few shrimps (prawns) for the garnish.

2 Mix the remaining shrimps (prawns) with the mayonnaise, soured cream or yoghurt and lemon juice. Season to taste.

3 Butter the slices of bread and divide the shrimp mixture between the slices to cover each slice evenly.

4 Whisk the egg whites until they stand in stiff peaks. Fold in the grated cheese. Spread the egg and cheese mixture onto the bread, being sure to completely cover the shrimp and mayonnaise mixture.

5 Place on a baking sheet and cook in the oven for about 20–25 minutes until golden brown.

6 Transfer to a warmed serving plate, garnish with the reserved shrimps and the parsley sprigs and serve while still hot.

LIGHT OPTIONS

If you are keeping an eye on your weight, try substituting low-calorie mayonnaise and low-fat yoghurt or sour cream in this recipe. It still tastes sensational, without being too high in fat.

CHAPTER TWO

Vegetarian Sandwiches

Whether you need a light lunch for two to break the day, a tray full of hearty nibbles to serve with pre-dinner drinks, or a speedy yet sustaining snack to replace a main meal, a sandwich will fit the bill. Even with the need for a vegetarian option, the range and choice will still be wide. Sometimes a little extra ingenuity is called into play, but that just adds to the excitement and novelty of the combinations possible.

Natural filling ingredients include cheese (and now there are so many vegetarian types available from Cheddar to Mozzarella); salad leaves in all their guises from mild corn salad to sharp, pungent radicchio; rich, sweet tomatoes from the minature cherry size to the hand-sized 'beef' (so perfect for slicing thickly); Mediterranean-style vegetables such as peppers, onion, courgettes, aubergines and fennel; eggs, hard-boiled and sliced, chopped and made creamy with mayonnaise or scrambled with asparagus, mushrooms or peppers; nuts, seeds and sprouts to give a munch and a crunch to a creamy or smooth filling; and grapes, apples, pears, bananas and luscious peaches or nectarines to give a fruity lift.

Choose breads that interest too: nutty and seeded varieties or flavoured types made with onion, cheese, olives or herbs. Then stuff fit-to-burst with an imaginative filling from the selection here.

Opposite: *Crispy vegetables and sweet, crunchy fruit make a myriad of delicious vegetarian fillings.*

STEP 1

STEP 3

STEP 4

STEP 5

GREEK FETA CROUTES

This is a wonderfully colourful and aromatic hot sandwich idea that makes a good first course or light lunch dish. For authenticity try to use Greek Halloumi or feta cheese.

SERVES 4

150 ml/¹/₄ pint/²/₃ cup olive oil
1 large clove garlic, crushed
1 tsp chopped fresh thyme
1 tbsp lemon juice
salt and pepper
1 small aubergine (eggplant), sliced, then cut into bite-sized pieces
1 large courgette (zucchini), thickly sliced
1 small bulb fennel, sliced and cut into bite-sized chunks
1 small red pepper, cored, seeded and cut into pieces
1 small yellow pepper, cored, seeded and cut into pieces
1 onion, cut into thin wedges
4 large thick slices country-style white crusty bread
100 g/4 oz Greek cheese (Halloumi or feta, for example), sliced or broken into pieces
8 black olives, stoned and cut into strips

1 Beat the oil with the garlic, thyme, lemon juice, and salt and pepper to taste in a large bowl.

2 Add the prepared aubergine (eggplant), courgette (zucchini), fennel, peppers and onion, mixing well. Cover and leave to stand for about 1 hour, stirring occasionally.

3 Spread the vegetable mixture on a grill pan or baking sheet with upturned edges. Cook under a preheated moderate grill (broiler) for about 15 minutes, turning over frequently, until the vegetables are tender and lightly charred around the edges. Keep warm.

4 Meanwhile, brush the bread with a little of the cooking juices from the vegetables and toast lightly on both sides until just crisp and golden.

5 Top each slice of bread with the cheese slices or pieces, then cover in turn with a generous amount of the cooked vegetable mixture.

6 Return to the grill (broiler) and cook for a further 3–5 minutes or until the cheese is bubbly. Serve at once garnished with the black olive strips.

BUCK RAREBIT

If Welsh Rarebit makes a delicious snack, then Buck Rarebit makes a complete sandwich style meal!

STEP 1

SERVES 6

50 g/2 oz/¼ cup butter
6 tomatoes, halved
175 g/6 oz/3 cups mushrooms, wiped clean
   and halved
6 eggs
6 slices of bread
100 g/4 oz/1 cup Cheddar cheese, grated
50 g/2 oz/½ cup fresh Parmesan cheese,
   grated
salt and pepper
pinch of mustard powder
5 tbsp milk

1 Put a knob of butter on each tomato half and each mushroom and cook slowly under a preheated grill (broiler) for about 4–5 minutes until cooked. Keep warm.

2 Poach the eggs in gently simmering water until just cooked. Remove from the heat and keep warm.

3 Meanwhile, toast the bread and remove the crusts if preferred. Spread lightly with the remaining butter.

4 Mix the Cheddar with the Parmesan cheese, season to taste with salt and pepper, then add the mustard powder and milk, stirring well to make a thick paste.

5 Spread the paste onto the toast. Place the toast slices on a rack under a preheated moderate grill (broiler), and cook until golden and bubbly, about 3–5 minutes.

6 Transfer the slices of toast to warmed serving plates. Top each slice with a poached egg and garnish with the halved tomatoes and mushrooms. Serve at once.

STEP 2

STEP 4

FOR GARLIC LOVERS

If you can't resist adding garlic to savoury dishes, try making your Buck Rarebit using butter mixed with a clove of crushed garlic. Simply use it instead of plain butter on the tomatoes and mushrooms and when buttering the bread.

STEP 6

STEP 1

STEP 3

STEP 4

STEP 6

SALAD DAYS

*When the sun is sizzling high in the sky, a light salad sandwich is
sometimes all appetites can cope with.*

SERVES 1

25 g/ 1 oz/ 2 tbsp butter
1 tsp snipped fresh chives
1 tsp lemon juice
4 slices granary bread
a little shredded crisp lettuce
2 hard-boiled eggs
2 tbsp mayonnaise or natural fromage frais
½ avocado, stoned
salt and pepper

1 Beat the butter with the chives and half of the lemon juice to make a smooth spread.

2 Spread the slices of bread with the prepared chive butter, then cover two slices with shredded lettuce.

3 Shell and chop the hard-boiled eggs and place in a bowl with the mayonnaise or fromage frais and mix gently to coat.

4 Peel and stone the avocado, cut into chunky slices or bite-sized cubes and toss with the remaining lemon juice to prevent discoloration.

5 Add the avocado to the egg mixture and fold gently to mix.

6 Spoon the mixture onto the shredded lettuce and place the remaining slices of bread on top. Press lightly to seal, then cut into halves or quarters to serve.

VARIATIONS

Avocado adds a creamy texture to this filling, as well as colour, but it is loaded with calories. For a low-fat option, replace it with two finely chopped potatoes and use low-fat yoghurt instead of mayonnaise. For a crunchy texture, add a very finely chopped celery stick.

In this recipe, you can make good use of the wide variety of crisp lettuce and salad greens now on the market. Crisp Cos, Webbs or Iceberg lettuce are natural choices but also consider shredded Chinese cabbage; slightly bitter or crisp Radicchio; curly feuille de chêne, frisée or escarole; flavoursome watercress or mustard and cress; and wild or red chicory, purslane, dandelion or burnet.

STEP 2

STEP 3

STEP 4

STEP 5

CIABATTA PIZZA TOASTS

Italian ciabatta bread is a floury, rough textured bread that makes the perfect base for a pizza-style sandwich dish.

SERVES 2-4

1 ciabatta loaf
6 tbsp/$^1/_2$ cup sun-dried-tomato and herb
  spread
150 g/5 oz/$^2/_3$ cup Cheddar cheese, roughly
  grated
1 red onion, sliced
225 g/8 oz tomatoes, sliced
100 g/4 oz mozzarella cheese, sliced quite
  finely
fresh basil sprigs, to garnish

1 Heat the oven to 220°C, 425°F, Gas mark 7. Split the ciabatta loaf in half lengthways.

2 Spread the sun-dried-tomato and herb paste evenly over both of the cut surfaces of the loaf.

3 Top the sun-dried-tomato and herb paste with the grated Cheddar cheese, followed by the red onion separated into rings, tomatoes, and finally the sliced mozzarella cheese.

4 Place both halves of the loaf on a large baking sheet and cook in the oven for 10–15 minutes, or until it is browned and crisp on top, and the cheese is bubbling.

5 Remove from the oven and garnish with the basil sprigs.

6 Cut into thick slices or leave in halves to serve.

QUICK TOPPINGS

The joy of this recipe is that it uses a prepared spread from the supermarket, so it is very quick to prepare. This example uses ready-prepared chopped sun-dried tomatoes with herbs and oil as its base, but this can be replaced with pesto sauce for a more gutsy flavour. You can also use a prepared tomato sauce with garlic and herbs. Look at the delicatessen section of your supermarket for other ideas.

STEP 1

STEP 3

STEP 4

STEP 6

WALNUT FINGER SANDWICH

Even the simplest sandwiches can be given a new twist if you make them with an unusual bread. The recipe filling below goes admirably with a nut bread like walnut.

SERVES 1

25 g/1 oz/2 tbsp butter or margarine
1 tsp finely grated onion
½ tsp snipped chives or chopped fresh
   parsley
salt and pepper
4 slices walnut bread
75 g/3 oz Roquefort cheese
about 6 black grapes
sprigs of parsley or watercress to garnish,
   if liked

1 Beat the butter with the grated onion and parsley or chives to make a smooth spread. Season to taste with salt and pepper.

2 Spread the slices of bread with the prepared butter.

3 Slice the Roquefort cheese thinly and layer the cheese onto two of the slices of bread so that the pieces of cheese overlap slightly.

4 Halve the grapes and remove any seeds. Place on top of the cheese slices, cut sides down.

5 Cover with the remaining slices of bread and press gently to seal.

6 Cut into thick finger sandwiches to serve. Garnish with parsley or watercress, if liked.

A blue cheese is the best companion for the nutty bread and grapes in this recipe. If you do not like blue cheese, replace it with a hard cheese with a sharp flavour, such as Leicester.

NEW BREADS

These days, supermarket shelves and bakeries all boast imaginative varieties of bread, from simple onion, nut and seeded to special olive and sun-dried-tomato studded types.

VEGETARIAN MUNCH AND CRUNCH

Vegetarian lunch-boxes needn't resemble rabbit-food boxes if a selection of fruit, vegetables and dairy products is mixed imaginatively. The recipe below produces a sandwich with lots of munch and crunch!

STEP 1

MAKES 2

50 g/2 oz smooth peanut butter
50 g/2 oz/¼ cup cream cheese
1 small carrot
1 celery stick
4 green olives
small handful of alfalfa sprouts or
    beansprouts
½ small red apple
2 tsp lemon juice
2 large wholemeal rolls or baps (buns)

1 In a small bowl mix the peanut butter with the cream cheese to make a smooth spread.

2 Grate the carrot, finely chop the celery and dice the olives. Add to the spread and, using a wooden spoon, mix gently but thoroughly to combine.

3 Place the alfalfa sprouts or beansprouts in another bowl. Core but do not peel the apple, then dice. Add to the sprouts with the lemon juice and toss well to mix.

4 Cut the rolls or baps (buns) in half and spread each half generously with the vegetable, peanut butter and cream cheese mixture.

5 Top each roll with half of the sprout-and-apple mixture, replace the lids and press gently to seal.

6 Wrap in foil to transport in a lunch box if required.

STEP 2

STEP 3

ALTERNATIVES

For a change, try replacing butter with other spreads such as mayonnaise, proprietary sandwich spreads, savoury pastes or spreads, bouillon-based spreads or well-seasoned vegetable purées.

Any number of different fruits can be used in this sandwich filling to produce a delicious variation on a theme. Consider adding diced pear, snipped dried apricot, diced fresh peach or nectarine, chopped fresh apricot or chopped banana to the sprout mixture instead of diced apple.

STEP 5

CHAPTER THREE

Big & Filling Sandwiches

It is generally recognized that the sandwich is universal and that every country, even every region, seems to have its own sandwich creation. It is hardly surprising, since the early origins of sandwich fare lie in the roots of peasant food. They may differ appreciably in their contents but all have one underlying theme – they are big, hearty, filling and generously-filled.

Most, such as the French Pan Bagnat, the Swedish Landganger (an open sandwich made on the spot by Swedish farm labourers), the American Club Sandwich and the Irish Bookmaker's Sandwich, use local and inexpensive ingredients and follow fairly specific guidelines on preparation. Others – such as the Yorkshire Chip Butty, the Liverpudlian Jam Sandwich and the Devonshire Clotted Cream Tea, have been devised with speed in mind.

Many of these are the sandwiches to prepare to replace a main meal dish. Hearty sandwiches don't necessarily mean door-stop-sized wedges of bread, although some are sliced generously, but the fillings are always on the heavy side. Many are better served with a knife and fork although that can destroy the spirit of the informal meal. These are also the sandwiches to take on picnics – fresh air definitely sharpens appetites.

Opposite: Hearty sandwiches made from a range of delicious breads provide a mouth-watering alternative to a main meal dish.

STEP 1

STEP 3

STEP 4

STEP 5

NICOISE (PROVENCAL) SANDWICH

This is a rough peasant sandwich particularly well known in the South of France in the Provence or Côte d'Azur region.

SERVES 2

1 French loaf, ideally round, about 18 cm/7
   inches in diameter
1 clove garlic, cut in half
5 tbsp olive oil
4 firm tomatoes, sliced
$^1/_2$ green pepper, cored and sliced
50 g/2 oz canned anchovy fillets
50 g/2 oz canned tuna, flaked
4 black or green olives, stoned
2 tsp capers
salt and pepper
1 tbsp lemon juice or wine vinegar

1 Cut the bread in half horizontally and rub the cut surfaces with the clove of garlic.

2 Sprinkle about 3 tablespoons of the olive oil over each bread half, drizzling it lightly but evenly over the surfaces.

3 Top the base with the sliced tomatoes. Arrange the pepper slices, anchovy fillets, tuna, olives and capers on top, then season to taste with salt and pepper.

4 Beat the remaining oil with the lemon juice or vinegar to make a dressing and sprinkle over the top of the sandwich filling.

5 Place the remaining bread half on top of the filling and press down lightly so that the juices mix.

6 Leave to stand for 30 minutes before slicing to serve.

ORIGINS OF THE NICOISE

The niçoise sandwich is derived from the days when peasants simply soaked their bread in oil and vinegar and filled it with an assortment of salad ingredients not unlike Salade Niçoise. This 'sandwich of the people' is also known as Pan Bagnat.

BOOKMAKER'S SANDWICH

This is a mammoth sandwich of cold steak and mustard in a Vienna or Danish loaf. It is so called because in Ireland bookmakers would take it to race meetings for a good satisfying lunch.

STEP 1

SERVES 4

1 long crusty Vienna or Danish loaf
100 g/4 oz/¹/₂ cup butter
675 g/1¹/₂ lb fillet, rump or sirloin steak, cut 2.5 cm/1 inch thick
salt and pepper
3 tbsp/¹/₄ cup horseradish mustard (or see boxed note below for alternatives)
small sprigs of watercress to garnish (optional)

1 Slice the loaf in half lengthways and butter it thickly.

2 Grill the steaks under a very hot grill (broiler) for 2–3 minutes on each side, according to whether you would prefer your steaks to be rare, medium or well-done.

3 Place the hot steaks on one half of the loaf. Sprinkle with salt and pepper to taste.

4 Spread the mustard over the meat, then top with the remaining loaf half. Press down lightly to seal the sandwich and enclose the meat.

5 Wrap the loaf in foil, then set it aside until the meat is completely

cold. (By wrapping the loaf, you will ensure that the meat doesn't dry out.)

6 Slice the sandwiched loaf into wedges for serving, garnished with watercress sprigs, if liked.

STEP 4

STEP 5

STEP 6

HERB AND PEPPER ALTERNATIVES

Although horseradish is the classic flavouring for the mustard used with this sandwich, you might like to experiment with other tastes: there are also prepared mustards available that are flavoured with thyme, tarragon and other herbs.

For a steak sandwich with extra kick, prepare the steak *au poivre* before grilling. About one hour before grilling, press 2 tbsp crushed black peppercorns (use a rolling pin for crushing) well into the steaks with the palm of your hand. Leave in a cool place until ready to cook.

STEP 1

STEP 3

STEP 4

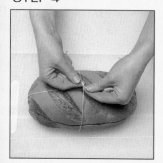

STEP 5

PICNIC SANDWICH

This loaf is cooked complete with its filling of tasty sausage meat, tongue and hard-boiled eggs. It is perfect to pack and take along on a picnic, for sandwiches that need no extra attention.

SERVES 8

1 small uncut bloomer loaf
75 g/ 3 oz/ 6 tbsp butter, melted
225 g/ 8 oz/ 1 cup pork sausage meat
100 g/ 4 oz/ $^1/_2$ cup cooked tongue, diced
1 small onion, finely chopped
2 eggs
150 ml/ $^1/_2$ pint/ $^2/_3$ cup milk
2 hard-boiled eggs, shelled and halved
salt and pepper

1 Heat the oven to 200°C, 400°F, Gas Mark 6. Cut horizontally across the loaf, two-thirds of the way up. and remove the 'lid'. Gently ease away the bread from around the edge of the crust. Make 100 g/ 4 oz/ 2 cups breadcrumbs from the bread.

2 Brush the cavity of the loaf and the lid with some of the melted butter.

3 Combine the sausage meat with the diced tongue, breadcrumbs and onion, mixing together well. Beat the eggs and milk together and stir into the meat mixture.

4 Place one-third of the filling in the bread case and arrange the halved hard-boiled eggs on top. Season to taste with salt and pepper. Pack the bread case with the remaining filling, then top with the bread lid.

5 Secure the loaf in a parcel-like fashion with string. Use the remaining butter to brush all over the loaf. Place on a baking sheet and cook in the oven for 15 minutes.

6 Cover the entire loaf with foil and continue to cook for a further 45 minutes. Remove and allow to cool. When cool, remove the string and cut into thick slices to serve. If you are packing this sandwich for a picnic, leave it unsliced and prepare it on the spot.

MEAT MAGIC

This sandwich idea has endless variations if you use flavoured sausagemeat to ring the changes in the basic recipe. Some enterprising butchers now offer varieties such as apple and pork, beef and tomato, pork and leek and variations of spiced and plain ingredients.

STEP 2

STEP 3

STEP 4

STEP 6

SAVOURY CHEESE FLUFFS

This is a variation of the definitive gentleman's savoury snack, stewed cheese, but made lighter and fluffier with the addition of egg whites. It makes a most comforting tea time or light meal.

SERVES 2

2 slices of toasted bread
15 g/ ½ oz butter or margarine
50 g/ 2 oz Cheddar or Lancashire cheese, grated
2-3 tablespoons thick double (heavy) cream
¼ teaspoon mustard
1 tablespoon snipped chives
salt and pepper
1 egg white
sprigs of parsley and tomato wedges, to garnish (optional)

1 Coat the slices of toasted bread with the butter or margarine, spread thinly.

2 Mix the cheese with the cream, mustard, snipped chives and salt and pepper to taste.

3 Whisk the egg white until it stands in stiff peaks then fold into the cheese mixture with a metal spoon.

4 Pile the mixture evenly over the prepared toast slices.

5 Cook under a preheated low to moderate grill until the topping is golden and fluffy.

6 Serve at once, garnished with parsley sprigs and tomato wedges, if you like.

Like many hot sandwiches, this one is best eaten immediately; it quickly goes limp and the cheese filling will lose its fluffiness if left.

SOFT BUTTER

Before spreading butter, let it stand at room temperature for 30 minutes or so before sandwich preparation (although there are now some varieties of butter that claim to spread 'straight from the refrigerator'). Alternatively, cream in a bowl until soft before spreading.

STEP 1

STEP 2

STEP 3

STEP 4

GRILLED PITTA POCKETS

Pitta bread is a delicious flat bread that is found thoughout the Middle East and seems to have been made for stuffing.

SERVES 2

2 pitta breads
2 generous handfuls of mixed salad leaves
 (such as lamb's lettuce, frisée, rocket/
 arugala, endive and radicchio)
5-cm/2-inch piece cucumber
2 tomatoes
2 spring onions (scallions)
2 tbsp French or yoghurt salad dressing
50 g/2 oz/ ½ cup cooked cubed lamb
 (optional)
1 tsp chopped fresh mint (optional)
75 g/3 oz/ ¾ cup cheese, grated

1 Carefully cut an opening into the centre of each pitta bread but not through to the base. Open out the bread pockets by gently pulling the bread apart.

2 Wash and tear the salad leaves into small pieces. Slice the cucumber, tomatoes and spring onions. Mix the salad ingredients together and toss with the prepared dressing. Add the lamb and mint, if using, and mix well.

3 Stuff the bread pockets with the salad mixture.

4 Sprinkle with the cheese so that the salad mixture is covered.

5 Cook under a preheated moderate grill (broiler) until the cheese is golden and bubbly, about 5–6 minutes.

6 Transfer to plates and serve at once while still hot. Serve with tomato and onion salad.

FILLING OPTIONS

Lamb is the natural choice for this sandwich because it is such a popular meat in Greece, Turkey and throughout the Middle East, where pitta bread is eaten several times a day. But feel free to make this filling with other meat. This is an excellent way to make the most of leftover roast beef or chicken. It would also be good with cold roast pork.

 To make your own yogurt salad dressing, beat 150 ml/¼ pint/⅔ cup natural yogurt with 1 tbsp lemon juice, 1 tsp clear honey, ¼ tsp mustard and salt and pepper to taste, until smooth and creamy. Flavour with chopped herbs, if liked.

STEP 2

STEP 4

STEP 5

STEP 6

SUPER CLUB SANDWICH

Club sandwiches are intended to be more or less adequate substitutes for a full meal and can be as many layers high as you can manage!

SERVES 1

3 slices white or brown bread
50 g/2 oz/¼ cup butter
100 g/4 oz crabmeat, flaked
3 tbsp lemon mayonnaise
salt and pepper
4 small crisp lettuce leaves
1 tomato, sliced
5-cm/2-inch piece cucumber, sliced
lemon wedges and watercress sprigs, to
    garnish

1 Toast the slices of bread on both sides until golden, then spread each slice with butter.

2 In a small bowl, mix the crabmeat with the mayonnaise, and salt and pepper to taste.

3 Cover the first slice of toast with 2 of the lettuce leaves, then half of the crab mixture and the tomato slices.

4 Cover with the second slice of toast, then the remaining crab mayonnaise and the sliced cucumber.

5 Place the third slice of toast on top, buttered side down, and press gently to seal.

6 Cut the whole sandwich into two large triangles or into quarters, and secure each with a cocktail stick (toothpick), if liked. Serve garnished with watercress sprigs and lemon wedge.

SANDWICH HISTORY

Legend has it that a man came home late and hungry from his club one night, raided the refrigerator and made himself a super sandwich, which he dubbed 'club'. Another says that the chef of a club made himself a reputation by devising a special sandwich. Either way, the club sandwich is now known as the king of sandwiches.

CHAPTER FOUR

Sandwiches for Entertaining

Everyone can recall the party when the canapés were too soggy or too dry yet few can recall super buffet sandwiches that were a joy to eat. Armed with the recipes in this section and a few useful tips you can stand unrivalled as the best party giver around.

If you need to make these sandwiches well ahead of a function, choose bases such as crisp toast or crispy baked bread. Top with a smear of butter to protect the base from moist fillings and toppings. Cover with cling film or foil to prevent drying out. Remember not to stack strong-flavoured fillings such as tuna and onion next to mild-flavoured fillings as they will absorb the flavour.

Danish Open Sandwiches are ideal to serve at a party as a varied selection can be prepared. The Scandinavians add interest by varying their bread from Danish to rye and wholewheat – many also use Scandinavian crispbread too. As a general guide, softer breads go better with firm toppings, for example tuna, salmon and salami, and harder breads go better with soft toppings such as cheese or eggs.

Sandwiches can also make a welcome entrance to the smart dinner party set. What could be more enticing at a lazy Sunday brunch than American-style bagels filled with smoked salmon, cream cheese and capers? Toasted goats' cheese on sourdough country-style bread with a designer salad and aromatic salad dressing makes a sophisticated starter to the chicest of dinner party meals.

Opposite: *Sandwiches with hot or cold fillings can play the perfect part in a summer evening supper party.*

STEP 1

STEP 2

STEP 3

STEP 4

PINWHEELS

These pinwheel sandwiches, filled with a bacon and tomato mixture and baked until golden, make delicious nibbles to serve with drinks. They are very tasty warm or cold.

MAKES 24

8 rashers streaky bacon
2 tsp oil
½ small onion, finely chopped
1 tbsp tomato purée
1 tsp yeast extract
4 slices of white or brown bread
15 g/½ oz/1 tbsp butter, melted

1 Heat the oven to 190°C, 375°F, Gas Mark 5. Lightly grease a large baking sheet. Remove any rind from the bacon and chop it very finely. Heat the oil in a pan, add the onion and bacon and fry together gently until cooked and turning golden but not brown, as it will be cooked further in the oven.

2 Remove the pan from the heat, then stir in the tomato purée and yeast extract.

3 Trim the crusts from the bread, then flatten each slice very lightly with a rolling pin.

4 Spread the slices of bread with the prepared filling. Roll up each slice widthways like a Swiss roll (jelly roll), then cut each roll into 1-cm/½-inch lengths. Secure with cocktail sticks (toothpicks). Place on the baking sheet and brush with the melted butter.

5 Bake in the oven for about 10–12 minutes or until golden brown. Remove the pinwheels from the oven and leave to stand on the sheet for 5 minutes until firm and set.

6 Transfer to a wire rack to cool further. Serve warm or cold.

FINISHING TOUCHES

Add a touch of elegance to a dish of pinwheels with garnishes. Little bouquets of watercress can be made by trimming the ends of a small bunch fairly short. Arrange these around the edges of a plate to give it a fresh and inviting appearance.

STEP 1

STEP 3

STEP 5

STEP 6

HARLEQUIN BUFFET SANDWICH

These sandwiches look so elegant at a formal buffet. Made from brown and white breads, they are sandwiched together with three different fillings and then cut to give a harlequin effect.

MAKES 18

8 hard-boiled eggs
225 g / 8 oz / 1 cup butter or margarine
2 tbsp mayonnaise
salt and pepper
50 g / 2 oz / ⅓ cup peeled prawns or shrimps
juice of ½ lemon
2 tsp tomato purée
1 tsp Worcestershire sauce
50 g / 2 oz liver pâté
6 slices brown bread
6 slices white bread

1 Shell the eggs and separate the yolks from the whites. Sieve the egg yolks and, separately, chop the whites very finely.

2 In a bowl, cream together 55 g/ 2 oz/¼ cup of the butter with the egg yolks, mayonnaise and salt and pepper to taste. Divide the mixture into 3 portions.

3 Finely chop the prawns or shrimps, add the lemon juice and half the chopped egg white and mix with one-third of the creamed egg mixture. Save the remaining egg whites and use them later in another recipe, or discard them if they won't be needed..

4 Stir the tomato purée and Worcestershire sauce into another third of the creamed egg, butter and mayonnaise mixture.

5 Mash the liver pâté and blend with the remaining one-third of the egg mixture. Butter the sliced white and brown bread. Using alternate layers of brown and white bread, sandwich together with the three fillings using four slices of bread per sandwich. Press well together, wrap in foil and chill until required.

6 Remove the crusts from the sandwiches and cut into 5 mm/¼ inch slices. Arrange on a plate to serve.

52

STEP 1 (BLUE BOY)

STEP 2 (BLUE BOY)

STEP 1 (COPENHAGEN)

STEP 2 (TIVOLI)

DANISH OPEN TRIO

*The Danish gentry originally were served their meat on slices of bread.
The meat was eaten but the bread was not – it was given to the servants.
Perhaps this is the origin of the Danish open sandwich.*

MAKES 3

*For all three sandwiches use 3 slices of
close-textured Danish bread, spread with
butter or margarine.*

BLUE BOY

*1 small lettuce leaf (one of the green
varieties, such as iceberg or butter lettuce)
3 slices blue brie cheese
3 black grape halves, seeds removed*

1 To make the Blue Boy sandwich,
place the lettuce leaf at one end of a
slice of bread. Arrange the slices of cheese
on the bread so that they overlap.

2 Garnish each slice of the blue
cheese with a black grape half.

COPENHAGEN

*25 g/1 oz roast beef, thinly sliced
1 small lettuce leaf
2 tsp mayonnaise
1 tsp fried onions
1 tsp grated horseradish
1 gherkin fan
1 slice tomato*

1 To make the Copenhagen open
sandwich, arrange the beef slices to
cover one slice of bread. Place the lettuce
leaf at one end of the sandwich and
spoon on the mayonnaise to secure but
not cover the lettuce leaf. Add a
scattering of onion and horseradish.

2 Position the gherkin fan opposite
the lettuce leaf and top the entire
sandwich with a tomato twist.

TIVOLI

*1 large lettuce leaf
4 slices hard-boiled egg
4 slices tomato
1–2 tbsp mayonnaise
15 g/^{1}/$_2$ oz Danish-style caviare or lumpfish
roe*

1 To make the Tivoli open sandwich,
cover the final slice of bread with
the lettuce leaf. Arrange the egg and
tomato slices in two rows lengthwise on
the lettuce.

2 Pipe or spoon the mayonnaise
down the centre of the egg and
tomato slices, and spoon the caviare
along the mayonnaise.

COUNTRY CROUTE

This is one of the simplest yet most sophisticated baked sandwiches – good enough to serve as first course at a smart dinner party. Remember, however, to use the very best bread, chèvre cheese, oil and salad leaves.

STEP 1

STEP 2

SERVES 4

4 thin slices of country-style French bread
    (sourdough for example)
4 small goat's cheeses or 1 x 125 g/ 4 oz
    chèvre log, sliced into 4 portions
2–3 tbsp olive or hazelnut oil
1 clove garlic, crushed (optional)
mixed salad leaves to serve (lamb's lettuce,
    frisée, rocket/arugala, endive and
    radicchio for example)
4 tbsp French dressing with herbs (either a
    good quality prepared dressing or your
    own blend)

1 Heat the oven to 200°C, 400°F, Gas Mark 6. Place the slices of bread on a lightly greased baking sheet and top each with a whole small goat's cheese or thick slice of chèvre log.

2 Mix the oil with the crushed garlic, if used, then drizzle over the cheese and bread.

3 Bake in the oven for about 10–15 minutes or until the cheese bubbles and browns on top.

4 Meanwhile, toss the salad leaves in the dressing and divide between four individual serving plates.

5 Top each serving of salad with a freshly baked croûte and serve while still warm.

A supply of croûtes can be kept in reserve in the freezer for later use. Drain the fried croûtes on absorbent paper and then pack them, interleaved with greaseproof or waxed paper, in a double layer of freezer wrap. Warm thoroughly when needed.

STEP 4

THE CROUTE FAMILY

Bread cut into various shapes can be used as a base for serving food – croûtes – or as a decoration – croutons. Croûtes can be used as a base on which to serve small game birds or noisettes of meat.

STEP 5

STEP 1

STEP 2

STEP 4

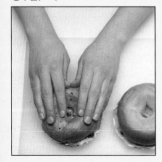

STEP 5

NEW YORK BAGELS

When a special Sunday brunch or lazy late breakfast is on the cards, nothing, simply nothing, is better than this cream cheese and smoked salmon bagel.

SERVES 2

4 plain or onion bagels
15 g/¹/₂ oz butter (optional)
100 g/4 oz cream cheese
1 tsp grated lemon zest
1 tbsp capers
a little shredded crisp lettuce (iceberg is best for this)
100 g/4 oz smoked salmon

Slice the bagels in half and spread with a little butter if liked.

1 Mix the cream cheese with the grated lemon zest, beating well until the mixture becomes smooth and creamy. Finely chop 1 teaspoon of the capers and add to the cheese mixture, mixing well to blend.

2 Divide the cream cheese mixture equally between the bagels, spreading evenly.

3 Cover the cream cheese mixture with a little shredded lettuce.

4 Cut the smoked salmon into thick strips and divide between the bagels evenly. Scatter the remaining capers on top.

5 Replace the bagel tops and press down on them gently to seal. Serve as soon as possible.

BAGELS AND SALMON

Bagels come in all guises – plain, sprinkled and flavoured with onion seeds, speckled with caraway seeds, and even studded with raisins and flavoured with cinnamon. Plain or flavoured varieties are also delicious with cream cheese alone.

Other cured or smoked fish can be used instead of smoked salmon in this recipe. Try using smoked eel, gravad lax (cured salmon with a dill coating), smoked sturgeon or smoked halibut. Thinly slice and cut into strips before adding to the bagels. Gravad lax strips can be topped with a mustardy dill sauce instead of capers, if you prefer.

STEP 1

STEP 3

STEP 4

STEP 5

CITY TOASTS

*This is an old Victorian sandwich recipe that will prove just
as delicious and popular today.*

SERVES 6

*100 g/4 oz/¹/₂ cup butter, softened over hot
   water or in the microwave*
50 g/2 oz/¹/₂ cup Gruyère cheese, grated
*50 g/2 oz/¹/₂ cup fresh Parmesan cheese,
   grated*
2 tsp double (heavy) cream
salt and cayenne pepper
*6 x 8.5 cm/3¹/₂ inch rounds (slices) of white
   or brown bread*
3 slices garlic, ham or liver sausage, halved
3 slices Gruyère cheese, halved
6 gherkins, to garnish

1 In a bowl, blend the butter together
with the grated Gruyère cheese,
Parmesan cheese and cream, using a
wooden spoon. Season the mixture to
taste with salt and cayenne pepper.

2 Lightly toast the bread on both
sides until golden and crisp.

3 Divide the cheese mixture equally
between the pieces of toast,
spreading lightly to cover.

4 Place a halved slice of sausage and
cheese on top of the filling on each
slice of toast, setting them at an angle so
that they look like 'wings'.

5 Slice the gherkins to make fans,
cutting each one several times
along its length without cutting through
fully at the end. Garnish each toast with
a gherkin, and serve.

A COFFEE HOUSE FAVOURITE

The name of these toasts derives from a
London tradition. Platters of City Toasts
were served at some of the most famous
City of London coffee houses in the 19th
century while the gentlemen guests
played chess.

Create variety by varying the garnish on
these sandwiches. Instead of decorating
with gherkin fans, try spring onion curls,
cucumber twists, carrot curls, sliced
olives, small tomato roses or herb bows
and bundles.

CHAPTER FIVE

Kids' Sandwiches

For lots of reasons – price, availability, choice and convenience – more children than ever are taking packed lunches to school every day. If your child takes a regular lunch box then remember to choose sandwiches that include as many of the basic food groups as possible, incorporating protein in the form of eggs, cheese, meat, fish, poultry or pulses; carbohydrate in the bread itself; fat in the form of butter, margarine or a dressing; and vitamins, minerals and fibre in vegetables, fruit and wholemeal breads. The recipe for Cheese and Apple Delights fits the bill admirably. Serve together with a glass or carton of milk or fruit juice and a piece of fresh fruit for a superbly well-balanced meal.

Kid's party fare is quite a different matter – the savoury sandwich selection must be appealing, especially if it has to entice children away from the sweeter offerings, but nutrition doesn't play such a vital role with such once-in-a-while treats. The emphasis here is on fun, attractiveness and variety. And what could be more attractive than an armada of egg filled boats set on a sea green layer of salad leaves or fishy slices of toast topped with letters to represent the names of the party guests (this also takes the guesswork out of who has eaten and who has not)! Fussy eaters will be enchanted with a game board pizza made with edible noughts and crosses on a crispy bread slice where everyone is a winner.

Opposite: *Fussy eaters will be enchanted with nutritious yet fun-to-look-at sandwich snacks.*

HOT DIGGITTY DOGS

Diggitty dogs are soft long rolls, spread with mustard, filled with a chilli onion garnish, then topped with frankfurters. They make wonderful barbecue fare – popular with children and adults alike.

STEP 1

STEP 3

STEP 4

STEP 5

SERVES 8

8 long, soft rolls or hot-dog buns
8 tsp mild American or burger mustard (or a
    hotter mustard for adults, if preferred)
8 frankfurter sausages or wienerwurst (see
    boxed tip below)
2 large onions, chopped
1 tbsp oil
1 tsp chilli powder

1 Cut the rolls lengthways, almost in half. Spread each roll with a teaspoonful of the mustard.

2 Cook the frankfurters according to the directions on the can or package, or, if fresh, drop into boiling water and simmer for about 5 minutes until heated through. Frankfurters can also be cooked in the microwave: place them on a plate and cook on high for about 1 minute.

3 Meanwhile, fry the onion in the oil in a heavy-based pan for about 10 minutes or until softened and cooked. Sprinkle with the chilli powder, mix well and cook for a further 2 minutes.

4 Spread equal amounts of the onion mixture into each roll.

5 Drain the frankfurters and add one to each roll.

6 Wrap the Hot Diggitty Dogs in paper napkins and serve immediately, while still piping hot.

DID YOU KNOW?

A long-standing rivalry exists between the *frankfurter* and the *wienerwurst*, both contenders for the title of original hot-dog sausage. The *frankfurter* from Germany and the Austrian *wienerwurst* are both lightly smoked. Traditionally they contain finely ground pork, but these days they may also contain beef.

Hot Diggitty Dogs taste delicious as they are but can be made extra special if you top with just a spoonful of tomato barbecue sauce. A quick and easy one is made by mixing in a pan 300 ml/ ½ pint/ 1¼ cups tomato ketchup, 25 g/ 1 oz/ 2 tsp butter, ¼ tsp chilli powder, 3 tbsp vinegar, 1 tsp brown sugar, ½ tsp chopped mixed herbs and salt and pepper to taste. Bring to the boil and simmer for 15 minutes. This is a delicious sauce to also serve with barbecued meat, fish and poultry.

STEP 1

STEP 2

STEP 4

STEP 5

WAGONS ROLL

Here is a very simple, if unusual, filled brown bread roll idea that is very popular with children. It is also very nutritious, and ideal to pop in a school lunch-box.

SERVES 1

2 round brown bread rolls
25 g / 1 oz / 2 tbsp butter or margarine
a little yeast extract
225 g / 8 oz canned baked beans in tomato
 sauce
1 tsp raisins
salt and pepper

VARIATIONS
Add a sprinkling of any of the following ingredients for a more 'adult' version of this roll:

grilled bacon pieces
chopped mushrooms
chopped cooked ham
onion, chopped and fried in butter

1 Cut the rolls in half, scoop out the soft bread from the top and bottom roll halves.

2 Make the soft bread that you have scooped out into crumbs by rubbing it against a coarse grater, then set it aside.

3 Spread the insides of the rolls with the butter or margarine and smear lightly with yeast extract to taste.

4 Mash the baked beans lightly with the scooped out and reserved breadcrumbs, then add the raisins, and salt and pepper to taste. Mix in any additional ingredients you also wish to include in the roll.

5 Pile the filling back into the roll bases, replace the lids and wrap in foil for transporting.

THE WHOLEMEAL OPTION

Wholemeal rolls are also ideal for this recipe. Wholemeal or wholewheat flour is made from the whole wheat grain which has been milled with nothing added or taken away. Stoneground wholemeal flour is much the same, but it is made in the traditional way using grinding stones.

EGGS AHOY!

These are miniature bread rolls that are perfect to serve at a children's party. They are fun to look at with their colourful and edible sails. Set sail on a sea of chopped green lettuce!

STEP 1

MAKES 12

12 small or miniature bread rolls
3 hard-boiled eggs, shelled
1¹/₂ tbsp mayonnaise
50 g/2 oz/¹/₄ cup butter or margarine
3 medium tomatoes
12 slices cucumber

1 Cut the tops off the bread rolls (forming a lid that will be used later) and scoop out some of the bread. Set the lids aside for the finishing touch.

2 Make breadcrumbs from the scooped-out bread by rubbing it along a coarse grater, or by using a food processor (a brief burst on high speed should be sufficient).

3 Chop the hard-boiled eggs and mix with about half of the prepared crumbs (use the remainder for another dish). Stir in the mayonnaise to bind the mixture together.

4 Butter the rolls then fill with the egg mixture and replace the tops.

5 Cut the tomatoes into quarters and remove the seeds. Place a slice of cucumber inside each tomato quarter.

6 Push a cocktail stick (toothpick) through each tomato quarter and cucumber slice, and use to represent a sail on each egg 'boat'. Serve as soon as possible to prevent the rolls going soggy. If ripe tomatoes prove hard to obtain, sails can also be made using a triangle of processed cheese.

STEP 2

STEP 3

PARTY CATERING

This is the perfect sandwich idea and the ideal opportunity to introduce mild herbs to children's food. Add 1-2 tsp chopped fresh parsley, chives or coriander to the egg mixture to introduce new flavours in a familiar format.

Under-six-year-olds may be overwhelmed by the sheer excitement of a party so that their appetites disappear. Older children, however, will eat an astonishing amount – at least as much as adults. Be sure to have enough food on hand!

STEP 5

STEP 2

STEP 3

STEP 4

STEP 5

GAMEBOARD PIZZA SLICE

This is a super idea for a child's quickly assembled lunch. Use a thick slice of bread from an uncut loaf for best results.

SERVES 1

*1 thick slice of bread
1 tbsp pizza sauce, tomato purée or tomato
    paste
25 g/ 1 oz/ 1/4 cup Cheddar cheese, grated
1 slice boiled or cooked ham
1 small tomato
1/2 green pepper, cored*

1 Lightly toast the bread on both sides until it is just lightly golden brown. (Overcooked bread will be too dry and won't 'take' the flavours as well.)

2 Spread the slice of bread with the pizza sauce, tomato purée or tomato paste.

3 Sprinkle the cheese on top to cover the slice evenly.

4 Cut the ham into long thin strips about 0.5 cm/ 1/2 inch wide and arrange on top of the cheese in a criss-cross pattern to look like a noughts and crosses (tic tac toe) grid.

5 Slice the tomatoes to look like the noughts (zeros) in a game, and slice the green pepper into thin strips so that two can be placed over each other to make crosses. Arrange a few noughts (zeros) and crosses over the cheesy grid (with perhaps a winning sequence!).

6 Cook under a preheated hot grill (broiler) until hot and bubbly, about 3–4 minutes. Transfer to a heated plate to serve.

EASY PIZZA SAUCE

The supermarket is a ready source of pizza sauces, but if you are so inclined, a fresh sauce can be quickly created using the microwave. Drain and chop a can of tomatoes, then place in a bowl with a little garlic, oregano and salt and pepper. Cook on high for 2½ minutes, stirring once. The sauce will keep sealed in the refrigerator for a few days.

70

STEP 1

STEP 2

STEP 4

STEP 5

INITIAL ANSWERS

In this recipe slices of bread are topped with a tasty sardine or mackerel mixture, then topped with initials cut out from cheese slices. They make good party-time sandwiches for children.

MAKES 4

4 slices Cheddar cheese
100 g/4 oz canned sardines or mackerel, drained
5-cm/2-inch piece cucumber, very finely chopped
¹/₄ small red pepper, cored, seeded and finely chopped, or 1 firm tomato, chopped
1 tbsp mayonnaise or natural yoghurt
salt and pepper
4 small slices of white or brown bread

1 Using initial cutters or a sharp knife, cut 4 initials from the cheese slices to represent the first letter of the name of each of the diners. Gather together any cheese trimmings and chop them finely.

2 In a small bowl, flake the sardines or mackerel and mix with the cucumber, red pepper or tomato, mayonnaise or yoghurt, and salt and pepper to taste, mixing well. Add the reserved cheese trimmings and mix well.

3 Toast the bread on both sides until light golden brown.

4 Spread the slices of toast equally with the prepared sardine or

mackerel mixture, spreading evenly to the edges of the bread.

5 Top each slice of bread with a cheese initial.

6 Serve as soon as possible, ideally with a knife and fork.

INITIAL VARIATIONS

The initial idea can applied to other recipes, too. If you are cooking for non-fish eaters (particularly children), use cheese initials to top ham, tomato or pizza-style fillings.

The sandwich filling and cheesy topping described above also make a splendid topping for a pizza. For speed and convenience use a ready-prepared pizza base (about 23 cm/9 inches in diameter). Top with 4-6 tbsp tomato sauce, spread with the prepared fish mixture, top with the cheese initials and bake in a hot oven for 12-15 minutes, until hot and bubbly.

STEP 3

STEP 4

STEP 5

STEP 6

CHEESE AND APPLE DELIGHT

It is important that children who take a sandwich lunch to school receive the same nourishment as those who eat a good cooked meal. This recipe is carefully balanced to provide many nutrients.

SERVES 1

2 country-style bread baps (buns)
75 g/ 3 oz/ ¾ cup Cheddar cheese, grated
coarsely
25 g/ 1 oz/ 2 tbsp butter or margarine
1 green dessert apple
2 ready-to-eat (pre-soaked) dried apricots
(optional)
1 tbsp natural yoghurt or fromage frais
salt and pepper

1 Place the baps (buns) on a grill pan rack (broiler tray) and sprinkle with a small amount of the cheese. Place under a preheated hot grill (broiler) and cook until just melted. Remove and allow to cool completely.

2 Split the baps (buns) in half and spread both pieces with the butter or margarine.

3 Core the apple but do not peel unless necessary. Coarsely grate the apple. In a bowl, combine the grated apple with the remaining cheese.

4 Snip the apricots, if using, into small pieces with kitchen scissors and add to the cheese filling, mixing well to combine.

5 Add the yoghurt or fromage frais with salt and pepper to taste and mix well to blend.

6 Fill the baps (buns) with the cheese-and-apple mixture, pressing down gently to seal. Wrap tightly for transporting to school.

AN ENERGY LUNCH

This filled bap is the basis for a balanced children's lunch. Served with milk and a piece of fresh fruit, it provides an energy-packed and sustaining meal that will see your child through the afternoon.
Added interest, flavour and nutrition can be introduced to this recipe by using rolls that have seeded tops – such as cracked wheat, sesame seed, poppy seed, buckwheat or caraway seeds. Alternatively, sprinkle the rolls with a little grated cheese and grill until the cheese melts before filling with the cheese and apple mixture.

SANDWICH TECHNIQUES

Freezing Bread
Bread freezes extremely well and it is always useful to have a few varieties stored away in the freezer. Keep all bread in heavy-duty plastic bags or foil and seal securely. Label and freeze for up to the following maximum times:

Crusty Breads	2 weeks
Rolls	2 weeks
Sliced Loaves	1 month
Uncut Loaves	2 months

Thaw bread, still in its wrapping, at room temperature. Large loaves may take as long as 4 hours whereas rolls, French sticks and small plaits may take as little as 30 minutes. If you simply want to toast frozen sliced bread do not bother to thaw first – it will toast perfectly well from frozen.

Freshening Bread
Slightly stale bread can be freshened easily for same day eating. Place the loaf or rolls in an ovenproof airtight cake tin covered with foil or wrap completely in foil. Place in a hot oven (230°C, 450°F, Gas Mark 8) for 5-10 minutes. Cool the bread in the container. It is then ready for use. Slightly stale bread freshened this way will turn stale extremely quickly so must be used as soon as possible.

THE HISTORY OF THE SANDWICH
Legend says that in the first century of the Christian era the ancient Romans taught the early Britons how to make *offula* – that is, a combination of foods similar to what is now known to us as a sandwich. But when the Romans withdrew from England the *offula* was soon forgotten, and was not rediscovered until the eighteenth century. It has not been forgotten since.

John Montague, fourth Earl of Sandwich, is generally credited with the invention of the sandwich. Seated at a gaming table and loath to leave it even for food, he called for slices of bread with beef between them to be brought to him so that he might continue gaming with one hand while he ate his snack from the other.

It is unlikely that he was the first person to dream up this easy-to-eat, portable meal (the French say it had been peasant fare for centuries), but he probably made it acceptable. It would prove interesting to see the astonishment the lively Earl would display if he could see the development his invention has undergone since then.

THE BREAD
Bread is the major part of a sandwich, so make sure it is fresh. A new crusty loaf can be put in the refrigerator for a few hours to make it easier to slice. Ready-sliced bread is handy because you have a choice of thicknesses and the wrapping keeps it fresh longer.

To vary sandwiches use different types of bread. Some of the lighter rye breads are particularly delicious, especially those sprinkled with caraway seeds. Breads flavoured with nuts, olives, sun-dried tomatoes and herbs make a welcome entrance when mixed and matched with suitable fillings.

Types of Bread
Bread has been made for at least 8,000 years so it is not surprising that there are many varieties to choose from. Add to that the vast range of imported specialities and you can easily appreciate that the choices are wide and varied.

Brown breads These basically differ with the flour used rather than with their shape. Choose from wheatmeal, wheatgerm, wholemeal and stoneground wholemeal. Some brown varieties also have nuts and seeds added for extra flavour, nutrition and interest.

White breads This is made from milled flour where most of the bran particles have been removed. Some bleaching of the flour also takes place to give the characteristic white appearance. The choices here are also wide, as some flours are then enriched with vitamins and paradoxically some have bran added back to the basic mixture.

Crusty loaves These loaves are mostly made with white flour (although increasingly more with wholemeal, too) and open-baked on the floor of the oven to give a golden crusty casing. There are basically six main varieties of crusty loaf: the bloomer, coburg, cottage, Danish, French and plait.

Enriched loaves These breads are enriched in some way – by the addition of eggs and/or fat and/or milk –and include types of bread containing fruit and malt. They include fruit loaf; malt loaf (made with special malt meal, sometimes with added fruit); milk loaf; cholla (a version of the Jewish Ritriel Bread thatis enriched with butter and eggs); and Vienna (enriched with milk).

Proprietary breads These are white and brown breads made from special flours and recipes, and sold under brand names. They include bran loaves (available in both brown and white varieties); brown breads (some have added wheatgerm or malted meal, while others are made from branded flours); and scofa (bicarbonate of soda is used as a raising agent instead of yeast, and the bread is usually cut into quarters from a large, flat loaf).

Tin loaves This category covers all types of bread baked in tins or containers and incudes the Barrel, Farmhouse, Pan or Batch, Sandwich and Split Tin. The description refers to the shape of the loaf; many can be made with either brown or white flours.

Rolls and Buns
In just the same way as there are dozens of varieties of loaves, there are just as many varieties of rolls and buns. Some of the most popular include brown, crusty white, fruited, rich such as brioche and croissants), soft white and wholemeal.

Continental varieties
The last few years have seen a veritable explosion of interest in different breads and supermarkets have responded by stocking a wide range of specialities from home and abroad. Local bakers have resurrected many breads that were popular years ago and have also produced some new bread ideas. It is not unusual to see Italian ciabatta and olive-studded foccacia bread alongside French brioche and baguettes, or American cornbread and muffins rubbing shoulders with Jewish bagels, and home-made speciality marbled breads swirled with onions, cheese, herbs, sun-dried tomatoes and pesto.

With such variety no one should lack inspiration for creating a super sandwich!

BUTTERING
A sandwich should be really mouth-watering, both in appearance and flavour, no matter if it is just a bite or a meal in itself. This means that every stage of sandwich making should be carefully considered – especially the buttering.

Do not skimp on the butter – spread the bread or sandwich base right to the very edges because the butter adds flavour, helps to hold the filling ingredients together and acts as a waterproof coat and prevents fillings from soaking through and making the bread soggy.

Storing Bread
Keeping bread fresh depends upon several factors. Sliced, white bread, enriched doughs and slimmers' breads will keep fresh for several days, but loaves such as Vienna or French should almost always be used immediately. Other factors which affect storage include the length of time the bread was baked and storage conditions.

■ Ideally bread should be stored in a clean container. wash out bread bins or crocks etc. with hot soapy water every week. This discourages mould from growing.

■ Keep bread in a dry container at normal room temperature, making sure that the container allows the circulation of air.

■ Keep any wrapped bread stored in its wrapper. Any uncut loaves can be stored in a plastic bag but not tied so securely that air cannot circulate.

■ Contrary to popular belief, bread 'stales' more quickly in the refrigerator than at normal room temperature, so do not store it in the refrigerator.

Flavoured Butters
Flavoured butters add interest and perk up traditional fillings so make up a batch of them and store in the refrigerator for up to 2 weeks.

Mustard Butter Cream 50 g/ 2 oz/¼ cup butter or margarine until soft, then gradually beat in 1 teaspoon English or 2 teaspoons French mustard. Use in sandwiches containing beef, lamb, bacon, ham, shellfish, herring or mackerel.

Horseradish Butter Cream 50 g/2 oz/¼ cup butter or margarine until soft, then gradually beat in 2 teaspoons grated fresh horseradish or 1-2 teaspoons creamed horseradish sauce. If using ready-prepared horseradish then check the strength of your make since they differ widely from mild to very hot. Use in sandwiches containing beef, herring, mackerel or smoked trout.

Lemon Butter Cream 50 g/ 2 oz/¼ cup butter or margarine until soft then gradually beat in 1 teaspoon finely grated lemon rind or zest and 1 teaspoon lemon juice. Use in sandwiches containing fish, veal or chicken.

Alternatives to Butter

Ring the changes by experimenting with unsalted butter and using other interesting spreads such as mayonnaise, proprietary sandwich spreads, meat, fish, game and other savoury spreads, yeast extract and other bouillon-based spreads, peanut butter and well-seasoned vegetable or fruit spreads.

THE FILLING

Always fill sandwiches generously and do not forget the seasonings. Fillings should be more highly seasoned than the same ingredients without bread. If a smooth filling is used such as cream cheese or potted meat, leave it at room temperature for about 1 hour – it will then be easier to spread.

Remember, too, that diffferent tastes are obtained by spreading each filling separately. For instance, if you are using peanut butter and jam, the two flavours will be more pronounced if the peanut butter is spread on one slice of bread and the jam on the other than if the two were blended and spread on both sides.

There is a host of sandwich ideas in the recipes in this book, but for added inspiration, why not try some of the following additional ideas.

Banana Mash with lemon juice and single cream. Try adding desiccated coconut or tiny crispy fried pieces of bacon.

Beef Cut into very thin slices and use on bread spread with horseradish sauce or mustard. Try adding coleslaw, sliced gherkins or cucumber.

Blue Cheese spread on brown or granary bread. Try adding crisp Cos or Webb's lettuce, thin slices of apple or grated carrot.

Cheese Slice or grate hard types. Try adding pickle, mustard, sliced raw onions, tomato, ham, pineapple, chopped celery in mayonnaise, yeast extract, lettuce or cucumber.

Chicken or Turkey Best finely chopped and mixed with mayonnaise, soured cream, thick yogurt or natural fromage frais. Try adding flaked almonds, spring onions, pineapple titbits, sultanas, crisp lettuce or mustard.

Corned Beef Slice or break up by mashing. Try adding horseradish relish, chopped gherkin or capers in mayonnaise, tomato, coleslaw, parsley or chive butter.

Cream Cheese Spread onto bread or mix with flavourings first. Try adding chives, spring onions, dates, raisins, sultanas, celery, apple, walnuts, diced cucumber, prawns or smoked salmon, crispy fried bacon pieces or capers.

Egg Hard-boil and slice, or mash with a little milk, or scramble. Try adding chopped gherkin, peppers, diced prawns or smoked salmon, chives, parsley, curry powder, onion salt and cucumber.

Lamb Trim away any fat from thin slices. Try adding tomato, gherkins, mint jelly, coleslaw, orange-flavoured mayonnaise, shredded lettuce or sliced cucumber.

Liver Sausage Slice finely or spread. Try adding grated carrot, coleslaw, fine slices of raw onion or apple, gherkins or tomato.

Pork Dice or slice finely. Try adding shredded lettuce, tomato, apple sauce, pickle, chutney or pineapple in a thick mayonnaise.

Prawns and Crab Shell and chop. Try adding cream cheese, chives in mayonnaise, diced avocado tossed in lemon juice, crisp lettuce or anchovy butter.

Sardines, Tuna or Mackerel Drain and mash. Try adding lemon-flavoured salad dressing, tomato, crisp cucumber, lettuce or celery salt.

Salami, Ham or Luncheon Meat Slice thinly and try adding pickles, chutney, coleslaw, tomato, lettuce or cucumber.

THE GARNISH

Suitable garnishes or decorations for sandwiches add good looks as well as flavour – but they must be as fresh as the bread, the butter and the filling. Colours should be chosen to tone with both the food and its setting or serving dish, and the flavour should complement the sandwich base and the filling or topping.

Try using carrot curls and gherkin fans, which always stay fresh and suit both hot and cold sandwiches; radish roses or water lilies, which are most attractive on open sandwiches; celery curls and spring onion curls can add a dash of sophistication to the plainest of sandwich fare; citrus twists, lemon butterflies and cucumber pinwheels give colour and flavour to fish and shellfish; and pepper and beetroot shapes – but add these at the last minute just before serving to prevent 'bleeding'.

FOOD ON THE MOVE

Sandwiches make the perfect food for packed lunches for the office, factory or school – and, of course, they feature in alfresco meals.

For first-class results try to make sure that the packed lunch is as varied as possible. Combine different sandwiches in the same lunch box – easy if you have made a batch in bulk well ahead and frozen them. Remember to freeze only those sandwiches whose fillings freeze well, so forget salad, egg and avocado offerings. Alternate crisp rolls and fillings with soft breads and smoother fillings, and sweet with savoury combinations. Remember to choose fillings that are not too wet.

Packed sandwiches can spell delight or disaster depending upon how they are prepared and packed. Rigid containers will ensure that the sandwiches arrive in one firm, whole piece rather than squashed. Foil, greaseproof paper and cling film will stop any transference of flavour from one sandwich to another.

Finally, add a napkin – sandwiches may seem perfect in every way for the lunch box, but they can still produce sticky fingers!

Herb Butters

Herb butters will prove infinitely useful for adding to grilled meats, fish, game or poultry, cooked vegetables and, of course, for making sandwiches.

Green Goddess Butter Cream 50 g/2 oz//¼ cup butter or margarine until soft, then gradually beat in 1 teaspoon each of finely chopped tarragon, chervil and parsley, 2 finely chopped baby spinach leaves and 1 teaspoon finely grated onion. Use in sandwiches containing fish.

Watercress Butter Trim and wash 1 bunch watercress then blend or pound into a smooth paste in a pestle and mortar or food processor. Cream 50 g/ 2 oz/¼ cup butter or margarine until soft, then gradually beat in the watercress paste, a pinch of castor sugar, and salt and pepper to taste. Pass through a fine sieve if liked and use in sandwiches containing meat or fish.

Garlic Butter Cream 50 g/ 2 oz/¼ cup butter or margarine until soft, then gradually beat in 2 peeled and crushed cloves of garlic. Use in sandwiches containing steak and robust-flavoured vegetables.

Chive Butter Cream 50 g/ 2 oz/¼ cup butter or margarine until soft, then gradually beat in 2 teaspoons finely snipped chives and 1 teaspoon lemon juice. Use in sandwiches containing chicken, vegetables or meat.

INDEX